POEMS
BY AN OLD BEAR

BY ROBIN T. HARRISON

Written by: Robin T. Harrison
Cover by: Dee Hunter
Illustrations by: Gary Rainsbarger and Alexus Elaine Raisty
Photos by: Robert Jensen, Bill Dow, Scott Plummer, Jeffrey Archer, Britt Dietz, Robert Spellman, Lee Calkins, Dee Hunter, Peter Murray, Eric Van Gilder, Victor Archer, Marty Wolin and Susan Newman-Harrison
Designed by: Susan Newman-Harrison
Proofed by: Vicky L Flanagan

Library of Congress Control Number: TXu 2-399-896

ISBN: 978-1-7337293-9-0

POEMS
BY AN OLD BEAR

BY ROBIN T. HARRISON

TABLE OF CONTENTS

PHOTO BY ROBERT JENSEN

PHOTO BY SCOTT PLUMMER

Introduction

It seems to me that as we get older, and we see that there really is going to be a day when we are gone, many of us try to capture in writing our "life stories". We delude ourselves into thinking that someone will be interested. Nobody will. Oh, if one has had, for instance, a distinguished military career, or has done something really significant, like maybe invented video games or the light bulb, a few copies of the autobiography might be sold, almost always at discount. Of course if you are a major criminal, involved in politics, you will get a million dollar book deal with a New York publisher. But since the vast majority of us don't really do anything noteworthy, it is probably a waste of time and effort to pen an autobiography.

I entertain the lunatic miasma that I am some kind of poet. Of course, I am not. So, if you read some of "my" poems, you will immediately recognize that they are parodies on real poets' works. In what follows, I will try to indicate the poem and poet who inspired my scribblings. You would do well to go to the originals. I do hope that you enjoy these modest efforts.

PHOTOS BY BILL DOW

Rob Harrison, ZLIN 142C, 19th Annual Apple Valley Airshow, 2022, Apple Valley, CA.

My Life (So Far)

I have tried to capture some of the adventures I have enjoyed over the last, say, 65 years or so. This one, the style is my own.

When I look back to the mountain days
Rivers that crashed to the sea below
Forest trolls that hid in the haze
Fields of diamonds spread on the snow
Nights so dark I could touch the stars
Lonely fires along the trail
Sometimes I think if there is a God
He must have loved me really well.

When I think back to when I would race
Wheels spinning, dirt flying, noise and smoke
Driving all night to a forsaken place
Just to discover the bike was broke
Living right on the edge of death
Pushing it harder than good sense would say
Sometimes I think if there is a God
He must have been with me all the way.

When the roar of the engine rang in my ear
When my eyes turned red from the wind
  and the dust
And the flag came down, and the crowd
  stood to cheer
And the hard won trophies turned
  slowly to rust
And the places I'd ride with an old
  and dear friend
Were stolen by people who could never see
That God, if there is one, must surely intend
To love and preserve my buddies and me.

When I remember the ocean life
Dying suns flashing red and green
Mermaids and pirates and unending strife
In a fairy world no one else has seen
Forests of seaweed, chasms of coral
Sapphire horizons, ivory sand

Sometimes I think if there is a God
My life has been held in the palm of his hand.

When I fly over the years that I flew
Soaring alone through the crystalline sky
Turning and tumbling and learning to do
Things that no one had done before I
Looking straight down to a postage
  stamp world
Seeing straight up to where angels dwell
Sometimes I think that if there's a God
He must have loved me very well.

When I recall the family years
The tiny wet faces, the wondering eyes
The shouting and laughter and loving
  and tears
The seasons that sped by, my awful surprise
When children no longer, each went his
  own way
Each one so different, yet all three the same
Sometimes I think if there is a God
He has loved me much more than
  I'd right to claim.

When I reflect on the man that I've been
And the friendships I've won, and the
  friends that I've lost
And I revisit the places I've seen
And the tears that I've bought, and
  the price that they've cost
What a bargain I've struck, what a hand
  I've been dealt
What stories I've lived, and am able to tell!
Certainly, if there is a God
He has loved me much better than well.

Rob Harrison, ZLIN 50LX, Cable Airshow, Upland, CA.

The Old Airshow Pilot

Bob Hoover was one of the most celebrated pilots of all times. In an over-a-glass-of-wine moment, my late wife Kathleen asked him— "When should Rob quit flying Airshows?" Bob's answer—"He'll know."

I'm Rob, Rob the Tumbling Bear
Skillful and cocky and proud
Flying around everywhere
Always pleasing the crowd.

For more than thirty years
I've made thousands of fans and friends
It's hard to hold back the tears
Knowing that now it ends.

The airplanes sit patiently waiting
On flat tires, covered with dust
Aluminum turning to powder
Steel parts turning to rust.

They don't understand why I've left them
Idle, wasting away
They say to each other "It's lovely,
Why can't we go flying today?"

Once resplendent in glory
Once polished beautifully bright
I just can't tell the sad story
That they have made their last flight.

Time's a thief, it steals from us
That what we treasure the most
And now their once-proud pilot
Is little more than a ghost.

So when I make that final
flight to the sky in the sky
I'll ask God's permission to bring them
And by His grace, we'll still fly.

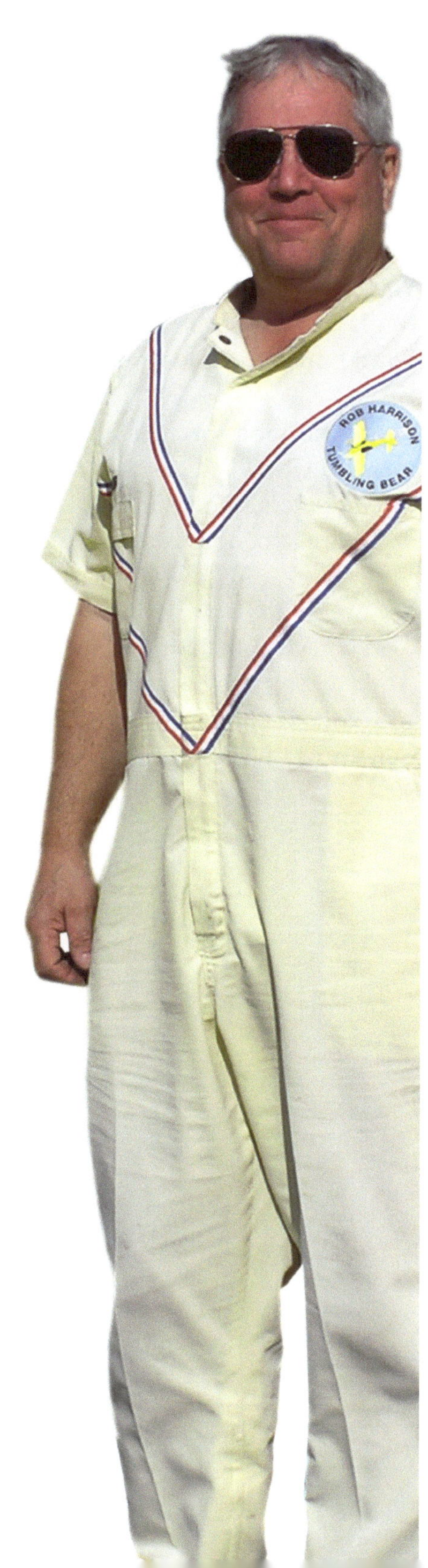

First Solo

I wrote this to celebrate my son's first solo flight. This event is a big deal to new pilots. The next few items are reflections on airplanes and flying.

There's nothing special about the sky
It's just a big layer of air
But if you could see into a pilot's heart
You'd find that the sky is in there.

There's nothing special about the clouds
You can watch them every day
But if you were to search for a pilots heart
You'd find that clouds are in the way.

There's nothing special about a plane
Rag and wood and tin
But if you could peek into a pilots heart
You'd find a couple therein.

For once you've pushed that throttle in
And you've pulled for an upward attack
And you've gone 'round the patch
  by your very own self
You know that you'll never go back.

Fog and Rain

IFR stands for Instrument Flight Rules. This means a pilot can't see where he is going and must depend on his instruments to maintain course and altitude. Thank you, Joni Mitchell.

Fog and rain and ice and snow
Crappy weather where 'ere I go
IFR, yes, but still I know
From clouds to stay away

I've studied clouds from up and down
From in the air and from the ground
And still when there are clouds around
The hangar is where I'll be found.

Reflections on Grounded Airplanes

Walk around any General Aviation airport on a pleasant Sunday afternoon. You will see airplanes covered with dust, sitting on flat tires, obviously neglected. Some of them have not been flown or even had their engines started in years.

And, you will probably see airplanes in hangars with open doors. Many are undergoing maintenance. Small airplanes demand an inordinate amount of attention, and most of the General Aviation (G A) fleet is more than 20 years old. Indeed, there are many airplanes from the '30s and '40s that are still on the FAA register and assumed to be airworthy.

In quite a few of the open hangars, you will see two or three old men, having a cigar or a cup of coffee or a beer. And telling stories; all pilots suffer from the incurable malady of needing to tell airplane stories. But if you look at the airplanes housed there, it is obvious that they haven't flown in a long time.

There are a lot of reasons why they haven't flown. Sometimes they need maintenance, or a part that is too expensive for the owner to afford, or is unavailable. All G A airplanes must undergo an inspection every 12 months, this is called an "annual". It must be conducted by a FAA specially certified mechanic. On the average G A airplane, the annual costs at least two thousand dollars, and often much more. So there are a lot of planes that are "out of annual". And there are additional required inspections and modifications, as well.

But the main reason these planes don't get flown is that their owner/pilot does not meet all the requirements to be pilot in command. There are lots of such requirements, and it gets harder to meet them as a pilot ages. One is a very rigorous physical exam, conducted by a FAA specially appointed doctor. Another is a Biennial Flight Review, conducted by a certified flight instructor. If the pilot wants to fly airshows, another annual check ride. Aerobatics just for fun, parachute must be re-packed every 6 months. For instrument flight, a check every 6 months. All this adds up to a large amount of money.

Most of these old pilots will never fly as pilot in command again. Most of them are constantly nagged by their wives or financial advisors— "Get rid of that airplane. Sell it. Give up your hangar. That will save us thousands of dollars!"

But they won't. And I understand why they won't. They can't. They say "I'm gonna go fly with Joe, and get my Biennial. Sam knows a doctor who will give me a medical. I will fix that defective magneto, with help from Mechanic Bill." But they can't.

So, why do they hang on to their airplanes, their hangars? Because they are PILOTS. Flying is a learned skill, an intellectual and physical endeavor. But it is also a life-long love affair, an affair of the heart. The old men can't face the awful truth, that they can no longer be real pilots. For any number of reasons; money,

physical infirmity, mental acuity. But, in their hearts, they are still pilots.

I have had the honor of working with many men of professional excellence. Engineers, who long after retirement still read all the engineering magazines and volunteered to teach at the local colleges. Lawyers, who long after retirement wrote legal books and did pro bono work. Machinists, who maintained their precision tools well-oiled and calibrated long after they had made their last cut on the mill or lathe. And so it is with pilots—airline pilots, fire pilots, airshow and movie stunt pilots, civilian commercial pilots, military pilots, G A pilots. Some can walk away. But some can't.

So I understand.

The PB4Y2 in war fighting trim.

Flight Test—PB4Y2

As Program Leader for Aviation at the U S Forest Service Technology and Development Center, and as a graduate Flight Test Engineer, it fell to me to test and approve newly modified airplanes that were going to be used as Fire Tankers. One such plane was a Consolidated PB4Y2, a four-engine "Patrol Bomber" based on the B-24. As manufactured by Consolidated it did not have enough power with the original engines to do our fire-fighting job, so Gene Powers, of Greybull Wyoming, undertook to modify it by installing more powerful engines. The plane soldiered on for many years dropping retardant on fires all over the U. S. But it became obsolete when the Forest Service started getting Lockheed C-130s for tankers. And appropriate Avgas was getting more expensive and harder to find. So the PB4Y2 found itself with a new assignment, going to airshows like Oshkosh, Chino, and Sun-n-Fun with the Commemorative Air Force. The pilots that flew the plane during its long and distinguished career fighting fire were the same ones that displayed it at airshows. I ran into them at the Chino show, where I performed in my Zlin 50, several years ago.

Of course engineering flight test can't be done by one person, so for the project I engaged the services of Dr. John Seevers, P.E., PhD, a veteran engineering professor and excellent pilot as well, and Eric Shilling, one of the original Flying Tigers, and a legend in the war-bird world. Here is a letter I wrote to the PB pilots—some history of the plane.

Woody and Bruce:

Having failed to find any engineering documentation of the flight test of the 4Y2, I thought you might enjoy the story version. As the poem starts, "A long long time ago, just when I quite forget..." I was assigned, as the technical advisor to the Interagency Airtanker Board, to do the acceptance flight of the airplane in question. To set the scene, you need to know a bit about the airplane's owner, Gene Powers, and the other people involved. I, the Program Leader for Aviation at the U.S.F.S. Technology and Development Center, at San Dimas, CA, was to be the star of this little passion play. It did not turn out so, but, more on that later. Dr. John Seevers, P.E., Ph.D. in engineering, accompanied. John and his then wife Melinda were under contract to do miscellaneous engineering work as assigned by me, because there was still a need for real engineering in U.S.F.S. Aviation, even though the T&D center was rapidly transforming to the "New Forestry", that it, forget science, it is all about politics and kissing ass of feminists, environmentalists, and trans-genders, and a bunch more deviates that I try hard to forget. The third member of our party was Eric Shilling. Eric was a Flying Tiger, an intrepid aviator, having flown the Hump in India, lived in I think it was Thailand, or maybe Nam or Laos or Burma, doing what I don't know, but having a great time. Eric wrote a book about his life, "Destiny", you can find it on Google. Maybe should this chronicle come to the attention of Rick, his son and now F.S. pilot, he could supply missing details. Eric, having thousands of heavy hours, was to be test pilot. John and I were to be flight test engineers (my Master's is in flight test engineering).

Gene Powers was a pioneer, innovator, and genuine good guy when it came to airtankers. A principal of Hawkins and Powers, Inc., a, if not the, leading natural resources flying contractor. Powers was to fly right seat, and be safety pilot. If bullshit were music, Gene would be a 100 piece orchestra.

Anyhow, one fine February, as I recall, morning, Eric, John, and I got on what I remember to be PSA, to Salt Lake, and on to Cody. From the very git things started to go to shit. The flight was late, SLC was having a typical SLC winter storm, with 0/0, 50 kts. We finally got into Salt Lake, about 4 hours late, and of course the commuter (maybe a Beech?) was grounded. Well, time for a little R&R, we would get there somehow. Eric accosted the little wimp behind the service counter for the airline, who had delightfully lacquered nails and false eyelashes, but apparently he identified as a male or something. Eric said that he was a decorated veteran, hungry, and the wimp's airline had made him late, and he would like please a voucher for at least a little snack. Fem-boy made the serious mistake of turning his back on Eric, while saying, "Oh, no, we just simply can't do that". Wrong thing to say, wrong thing to do. Did I mention that Seevers is about 6'3, 250, and solid gristle? He reached over the counter, picked up Mr. Fingernails by one arm with one hand, and said "I don't think you know who you are talking to."

After a nice meal, with wine and a view of the storm outside, it was announced that the flight to Cody would depart momentarily, and please would the three Forest Service Officials who had just been upgraded to first class mind please reporting to the gate please? So, we wobbled to the gate.

The flight to Cody was about as uneventful as might be expected, except for some tooth-jarring turbulence, and we were duly deposited on the tarmac at Cody. After what I thought was an impolitely long walk in the deepening dusk, especially since John and I were carrying about one thousand pounds of flight test instrumentation, we got to Enterprise or Budget or maybe Avis (The FS had a standing rule—Hertz is the most expensive—don't rent from Hertz), we discovered that, one, they were closed, and two, it didn't "mattah" (The parking dude—night watchman, who was not readily visible in the gloom), said "Cauz dey rent all da cahs anyhow" An annoyed if not downright abusive call the manager followed, threatening a visit from the FBI. Manager grudgingly trundled out with a Ford Fiesta. Scarcely the van we had reserved, but, we were on our way.

I was driving. I was exhausted. It was about 2000, and we had had nothing to eat but a bag of peanuts since our free lunch. I went to sleep driving, and after a memorable excursion across the Wyoming Tundra (John and Eric were asleep, as well), we finally arrived in the neighborhood of Greybull. For my readers who have never been there, don't go. The first thing that greeted our eye was a collection of what appeared to be cut-rate Washington Monuments, but turned out to be the tails of C-130s, strategically parked at wide spacing, apparently in case of Soviet attack. I dunno.

We entered Greybull, tired, hungry, and uncomfortable from an hour's drive in a very small auto, filled with gyros, clipboards, and the other paraphernalia that we needed to look like we at least pretended to know what we were doing. Parking, and walking to the entrance of the first diner we came to, a waitress that would have been right at home in Lake Woebegone slammed the door in our faces, "We're closed". I said "But Gene Powers told us to come here" "OH, you guys are with Gene? Come on in! What can I get you? Coffee, I have a fresh pot. Just made a cherry pie, I'll warm it up. How 'bout a chicken-fried steak? How 'bout some fried chicken? Corn and beans ok?"

After a truly excellent country meal, with Maude quizzing us re what we were going to do with Gene, and "ain't he the greatest guy, and I heard all about you guys, you are THE Eric Shilling, really? Can I have your autograph?", Maude called the Best Rest Motel, told Maude II that three very important government men, but nice, were coming her way. M II received us most graciously, and the rooms were clean, comfortable, and delightfully decorated with cows, bunnies, and airplanes.

The morrow broke clear, crisp, and promising thunderstorms by 1500. Back to Maude I, for a breakfast that would lead to an immediate heart attack now, the ham was to die for, I still remember it after probably 30 or 35 years.

And so to Hawkins and Powers, to test the Mighty PB4Y2, upon which Gene had installed Wright 2000 hp motors (Bruce, Woody, set me straight if I misremember).

The receptionist, though apparently expecting us, icily informed that "Mr. Powers is busy, he will see you when it suits him." Hmm. More things going to shit. We had a full card to fly, and, 1500 tsms.... We sat there, reading 3-year old Trade-a-Planes, when the chief mechanic (his name was Rennison, I think) carrying a 3350 master rod though the lobby, recognized Eric. "(Hey, this is Eric Shilling, the Flying Tiger! Hey, everybody, this is ERIC SHILLING!!). The commotion woke Mr. Powers from his nap, and he ambled out to the lobby. "Hi Rob, Hi John. I didn't know you were bringing the FAMOUS ERIC SHILLING! Hey Eric, I gotta show you some stuff. You guys go on out to the aircraft and get set up."

Now Gene Powers was the complete Airtanker dude. And by complete, I mean he had facilities to do ANYTHING on an airplane. He not only had facilities for airframe repair and mod, engine overhaul, and avionics installation and service. He had paint shops. He could hard chrome and grind struts. He could do every kind of non-destructive test ever invented. He had a HUGE stock of engines, airframes, obsolete radios, including,

I later found out, several fully functional (per Gene) A-N receivers for C-47s. And he had to show it all to his distinguished guest. And if Powers was an orchestra, Shilling was a brass band. The two got on famously, while the Project Leader (me) felt left out, got more and more nervous about the time/weather, and began to wish that I had gone to Julliard instead of Oregon State.

John and I sat on our thumbs until about 1400, when the first large drops of H20 splashed the cracked asphalt of Greybull airport. It was time to go fly. There are two doors on the PB4Y2, one in the fuselage, which is normally used by flight crew, and an emergency hatch above the pilot-copilot's heads. It is about 30 inches in diameter. Because the fuselage is full of tank (the development of which is another story), access is had only through the escape hatch. Access to the access is a few pieces of stainless round conduit tubing sheet-metal screwed to the fuselage. Slippery round stainless tubing. It began to rain some more. Eric started up first. Visions on my career being abruptly ending when this 70-year-old senior citizen slipped and broke his hip on the ground 23 feet below.

Eric got up just fine. BUT the hatch, as I mentioned above, is 30 inches diameter. Eric was 38 inches diameter. I was about the same. Seevers stood on Eric's shoulders and jumped up and down, squeezing him into the cockpit. I sucked it up and forced myself in. Gene was the skinniest of us all, he slipped right in, without Vaseline. Poor Seevers, whose shoulders were and still are about 4 feet across, tore all the hair out from one armpit. But we were all in, hatch locked.

John and I had already set up all our instruments, and so were ready to go. I sat in the flight engineer's seat, John on a jury-rigged jump seat. Eric was flying left seat, Gene right.

First thing Eric did was look over the check

list, and toss it aside. Gene said, slowly, "Now, Eric, to start the Wright, you..." Response– "I can fly the airplane, Powers. You shut up and pull the gear up on my command. Turning 4 out there...."

Off we went. First maneuver was a doublet, a rapid fore and aft pulse of the yoke. The idea is to set up a longitudinal instability, and count the "zero crossings". First doublet was a little mild, I didn't get a good count. "A little more vigorous, Captain", said I. The next doublet pulled about 8 gs, and we got lots of good zero crossings. Next a wind-up turn, a dangerous maneuver if done incorrectly or too low, because the airplane can depart, turn over on its back, and then we have real problems. This and all the following maneuvers, were accomplished beautifully, on altitude, on speed, on heading. Test pilots have a saying– "Card the flight, fly the card". John and I carded the flight, Eric flew it perfectly.

Last maneuver was a drop, using water instead of retardant, to assess the drop pattern. If you have never flown an Airtanker, you have no idea how difficult it is to get heading, altitude, and timing right. By now we had about a 30 kt crosswind, and lightning all quadrants. Drop was perfect, just perfect, so time to land. On final, Eric cut the outboards, and on touchdown, the inboards. Taxied right into the chocks, dead engines, landing and shutdown checklists complete, did a little bow, and stopped. "Wow, Eric, you fly this airplane pretty good!" said Gene. Replied Eric "It's no problem, Gene, I flew one in 1947."

One could have hoped the day's adventure might be over, but it was not to be so. Same storm doubled back, delays at Cody and SLC. Eric was all excited about the flight, he had had a really good time, and he and Gene vowed to get together soon. I don't know if they ever did, but I sure hope so, because if there ever were two guys that ought to be fast friends, it was them. John and I limply snoozed on the return leg, while Eric, I later heard, annoyed and propositioned all the stewardesses (That is what they were called then, and they were all very young and very pretty). After John and I staggered down the airstair at ONT, no Eric. "Well, whadda you know, he finally conked out." Not so—he was berating the flight crew "Now, son, if you would keep it spooled up over the outer, you can still chop close in and not land like you are flying a pogo stick...." "Yes sir, Yes sir" was all I heard for a reply.

Eric bounced down the airstair like he was 15, yelled over his shoulder "see you boys in the morning", and was gone before John and I could catch our breaths.

Eric died some 15 years after this, what was, I believe, his last official test flight. He and I continued a long and firm friendship, his boy Rick came to work for me at the F.S., Ilsa his stunning wife and my Kathleen became very close, and his passing ended an era that we are not going to see again. But of all the beer I drank with Eric, all the lies we swapped, all the good times we had, nothing stands out in my memory like the flight of the 4Y2 that stormy day in Greybull, Wyoming.

Gunga Jim

High performance cars and motorcycles have always been a major part of my life. I have raced profession-
ally with some of the best of the time, and even won a few main events. My business partner for many years
was the five times U. S. road racing champion. But of all my biking experiences, and they have spanned
the gamut from trials to road racing to flat-track and TT and desert racing, the most challenging was an
off-road ride led by Jim Williams. The poem is a parody on Rudyard Kipling's "Gunga Din". With sincere
apologies to R. Kipling.

You can talk of rugged rides
And of how you skinned your hides
And how your Radfuehrer's faster
  than the wind
But when it comes to crashing
And ugly mountain bashing
No leader gets a smell of Gunga Jim.

The Honda that he rode
Was really quite a toad
But it didn't mean a thing to Gunga Jim
For all their Husky class
Not one of them could pass
That asshole when the spirited haunted him.

Oh Jim Jim Jim
Here's a beggar witha bone stuck
  through his shin
He's sniveling and he's hurt
And he's rolling in the dirt
You'd better get the doctor Gunga Jim.

The weekend that we went
For Patterson's ascent
Was s'posed to be the easiest of cruises
But with rocks and heat and slopes
And a dozen dozer dopes
It turned into a massacre of bruises.

The first to crash was Rob
Well recognized a slob
Who rides 'bout like your average baboon
He hit the Fah King's tree
and bloddied up his knee
And swole his hand up like a red balloon.

Immediately Paul

Hit the same tree, did fall
Really did a number on his pinkie
Then Bob slipped on a rock
And damn near split his c***.
And snapped two leg bones
  quicker than a winkie.

Oh Jim Jim Jim
What's the matter with guys
  who ride with him?
The crash and break and bend
Never make it to the end
For God's sake slow the pace down Gunga Jim.

The wimps all left for home
Leaving Jim there all alone
So he thought he'd go and try it
  one time more.
He gave it one more go,
By God wouldn't you know
Got three toes on Hungarian Gabor!

So I'll meet Jim by and by
On that trail up in the sky
Where you can ride all day
  and never stop for gas
He'll be leading larger groups
Over mountains, over whoops
And I'll catch him, and
  I'll knock him on his ass!

Oh Jim Jim Jim
Not one of us comes close to
  catching up with him
We brag and we say we could
But if we could we would
You're a faster man than I am, Gunga Jim.

Ghost Bikers

Motorcycle people are among the most carefree and friendly and helpful folks anywhere. But the one thing they absolutely will not put up with is a complainer. Sung to the tune of "Ghost Riders in the Sky"

A dirt biker went out to ride, one hot and sunny day
He blasted up a sand wash as he went along his way
When all at once a noxious cloud of dust covered the sky
And he saw some riders coming down, and heard their mournful cry

Snivel eye aye, Snivel eye oh,
Wimp riders in the sky.

Their frames were bent, their rims were dent, their tires all were flat
Their handlebars were twisted, their exhaust pipes all went "blat"
They all had ugly bruises, and they all were cold and wet
They all said that they'd finish, but not one of them has yet

Whiners eye aye, whiners eye oh,
S*** bikes in the sky

As one of them rode toward him, his heart was turned to stone
He looked for his companions, but he saw he was alone
As the biker passed on by him, he said "buddy got a buck?
I've got to call my wife and have her bring the pickup truck."

Pussies eye aye, pussies eye oh,
Wimp bikers in the sky.

Now partner pay attention, 'cause I've got something to say
Nobody gives a f****** s*** 'bout how you feel today
So buddy quit your bitchin', or with us you will ride
A-pissing and a-moaning, across this endless sky.

Snivelers eye aye, Snivelers eye oh,
Complainers in the sky.

The Parable of the Three Bikers

I met three sojourners in a coffee shop. They were bikers, but they were sitting apart. In gentler days, one would expect to meet sojourners, in a roadside tavern, on foot, perhaps horseback or even snowshoe, but in these times, it is not possible to sojourn on anything but a motorcycle.

I asked the first where he had been" I dunno man." Then where are you going? "I dunno man." I said, "But if you don't know where you've been and you don't know where you're going, why are you...." But he had picked up his gloves, cranked his panhead, and cruised off down Main Street.

I approached the second: "What did you see? What did you hear?" "I saw mountains, and I saw rivers, and I saw oceans. I heard the sigh of the wind, the whine of the gears. I felt the hot desert air and the cool mountain breeze. I smelled salt and pine trees, the wetness of the woods, and the dryness of the desert." He was an aesthete wearing a Barbour suit and two-tone tan leather gloves with three elastic bands at the wrist. "Do you have pictures?", I said, "Can you show me a photo?" But he had mounted his Gold Star, leaned forward on the clip-ons, and with inside knee extended raced off with a lisping rasp of exhaust and a flash of light from the polished aluminum gas tank.

The third biker, I asked, "What did you do? "Oh," he said, "I rode here and there. I helped a lady change a flat. I stole some grapes and an orange, and I came here to have lunch." I started to ask, "How did you know.....?", but I saw that he didn't want to talk, and since his bike was only a V65, I didn't think it worth the effort to follow up.

Where have we all been, and where are we all going? The first biker, the Harley man, wouldn't say it, but he knew, just as we know. We are all going only one place, and that's the end of our journey. Does it matter where we've been? Does it really matter where we think we're going? There's only one destination for us all. The road we take to get there doesn't count for much.

What we see, hear, and feel along the way can make the journey pleasant or burdensome, but once we have set our course there really isn't much that we can do to change the sights along the way. We might see and hear and feel what's there, but what's there is there, whether we hear it and see it and feel it or not.

But what we do — ah, there's the difference. The tires we have changed, the oranges we've stolen; the sacrifices we've made, the selfish times we haven't sacrificed; the friends we've betrayed, and the betrayed that we've befriended; these are the markers, the counters, the notches in our stick that distiguish us all one from another.

It is within each of us only to regulate what we do, not what we see or feel, not where we've been, not even where we're going. When the markers are called, when the notches are counted, what we've done will be remembered.

The Butcher of Barstow

We used to be able to ride unfettered through all the deserts of Southern California. But with the rise of the religion of Environmentalism, more and more restrictions were placed on off-road vehicles, and the government bureaucracies that have charge of public lands have managed to exclude almost everybody from the lands that we are told we all own. One leader in the anti-bike brigade was an ecologist from the Bureau of Land Management. Like all good bureaucrats, she worked assiduously to steal our riding from us. Most of the desert is now closed in the name of "Preventing Ecological Damage".

So here is a tribute to one warrior who successfully destroyed an industry, and obliterated one more opportunity for families to recreate together.

Once upon a morning sunny
While I tried to spot a bunny
or some other mammal funny
hopping 'cross the desert floor.
Suddenly the pavement ended
and all the progress was suspended
For the tortoise was befriended
by the BLM's chief bore.

Blond she was, and rather pretty,
No one said whe wasn't witty.
But it surely seems a pity
that her focus is so small.
For this reptile dumb and lowly
has become her icon holy
"If desert's fauna's dying slowly
tortoise will outlast them all."

No more bikers, said Dr X****
Makes the lizards much too wary
And our rats find them too scary
They can ride some other trail.
No more miners, no more flyers
No more stringing power wires
No more things with rubber tires
Spare our tortoise this travail.

So the desert, it was taken
by fraud, and we did not awaken
until too late! All use forsaken.
Now the turtle's future's set
No one round to crush his shell
or otherwise to give him hell.
"Our job," she said, "we've done too well?
We need to find anothr threat"

"The raven, he might fit the bill
A raucous bird, well known evil
We can keep our jobs, friends, still
If we blame old Raven for
tortoise, tortoise dead and numerous
We will promulgate the rumorous
That these birds, bland and malfumerous
Kill baby tortoise by the score.

So poison we will plant in ova
And we'll go in our Land Rova
Over hill and through the clova
Spreading deadly eggs around.
Ignore the cats and dogs we kill
Or if we get some small peopil
Nothing feels quite like the thrill
of keeping desert tortoise sound.

This plan failed. The Audobon
cried "No birdies, not a one,
will fall by poison — we'll not run
from our duty to the raven."
But turtle's more important than
mere birds, or even mere man,
And so, while searching for a plan
She hit upon a scheme more craven.

"We will shoot them, bird by bird
We will make our logic heard
We will prevail, you mark my word
Not a raven shall survive."
Seems to me this pseudo-science
of BLM's Desert Alliance
And of all good sense, defiance...
Not one of <u>them</u> should stay alive!

Tribute to Stellantis Engineers

We are lucky enough to own a Jeep Grand Cherokee. The guys that designed and built this thing were genii! Snow, dirt roads, hills—No Problemo! Stellantis (Formerly Chrysler) engineers are the best! Bill's was the café where locals used to eat. Sadly it is gone now.

Oh Mr. Jeepely Jeep
Through the snow we creep
Up and down the hills
We're gonna get breakfast at Bill's.

Oh Mr. Jeepely Jeep
Sometimes you make me weep
Sometimes you give me thrills
On our way to breakfast at Bill's.

Oh Mr. Jeepely Jeep
Doesn't matter how steep
You have the driving skills
To get us to breakfast at Bill's.

Old Man Looking Back

Some days are bettter, some are worse. I must have written this on a bad day.

I hear a ringing in my ears
Most everything moves me to tears
I harbor the most awful fears
Will I see one more day?

All my joints radiate pain
I need new glasses yet again
My ankles are in constant sprain
I want to get away!

But still I labor hour by hour
Too many projects turn me sour
I just want to smell the flower
I want to go and play.

Old age sits quite hard on me
I think of what I used to be
When I was young and wholly free
And had it all my way.

Rob Harrison, ZLIN 142C, Apple Valley Airshow, Apple Valley, CA.

Rob Harrison, ZLIN 142C, Apple Valley Airshow, Apple Valley, CA.

Old Man Looking Forward

Faith sustains us. Works fulfill us. I try to have both.

Sometimes I wish I weren't so old
Sometimes I'd like to be less wise
It's hard to be still strong and bold
When tears keep popping from my eyes.

When I was young and lithe and bold
And the world before me lay

I never thought of growing old
and lying down to pass away.

But now the years that lie behind
are golden in my memory
And yet I look ahead to find
What lies ahead, what I shall see.

Beyond

I have no complaints about my life. I have done things that most people can never do. I have had love and hate, triumph and defeat, good times and bad. I have lost everything, and gained everything back. But, even now the wild, the unknown, the challenge, still haunts me.

What is beyond this mountain?
What lies across this sea?
Where does this unpaved road lead?
Is it somewhere that I'd rather be?

What keeps me from leaving?
Why am I staying here?
What are the losses for which I'm grieving?
Why is this place so dear?

If I could return just a short way
To before my life was not mine
To before my worries all held perfect sway
Over all of my time.

I'm useless, I'm nothing, I'm no one
Why am I being held back
By only my fears of being alone?
Why shouldn't I follow that track?

I would again walk and run
The lonely mountain road
Alone, with only me myself
Without this awful load.

My memories keep me from going
My past ties me fast to this place
My loves like a well-spring flowing
Prevent me to take up the pace.

I'll not know beyond the mountain
I'll never cross the sea
The road that leads to forest and fountain
Will remain untrodden by me.

But in my heart still I wander
The mountain, the ocean, the track
And I mourn for the loss of the long-gone yonder
And fervently wish to go back.

Summerhill

My wife Susan and I, and Little Bear the Dog, and Petey the Cat, live on top of a mountain in Lake Arrowhead, California. The builder/owner of the house christened it "Summerhill", so that name stuck. Being high on a hill, and close to the lake, it suffers greatly from the wild-wind winters we enjoy. A LOT of damage was done one particularly severe winter, and a local contractor was tasked to do the repair. John was his foreman. It was unseasonably hot when they were working. Read Robert Service's "The Cremation of SamMcGee".

There are strange things done
In the blazing sun
By the men of Arrowhead
And the mansions there
Will make you swear
And sometimes wish you were dead
When the fierce wind screams
And the water seems
To enter every crack
And the ceiling drips
And your footing slips
And you fall down on your back

Now the house I mean
Had a leaky seam
On every corner and wall
And I sometimes swear
If I weren't a bear
I wouldn't live here at all
But the view is grand
And I truly planned
To spend my last years here
So my bucks I spent
On a plastic tent
Inside, though it looked quite queer

The stalwart men
That would come back again
On every broiling day
Though the sun was hot
They worked a lot

And tore the siding away
The OSB
Had the smell of pee
It was rotten to the core
And the plastic deck
Just looked like heck
And there was a great deal more

But despite the heat
They would beat and beat
On the timber that needed new
To repair the break
That faced the lake
And they fastened it with a screw
Some planks they tore
From the office floor
And they moved all of our art
To the big garage
Where the Bentley lodged
On an improvised wooden cart

The tools we found
That were scattered around
On our deck destroyed our view
But the dudes that came
Every day just the same
Were making the house like brand new
They worked very well
And were really swell
And they stayed out of our way
I couldn't complain

PHOTO BY SUSAN NEWMAN-HARRISON

Though wracked by pain
At the cost I would have to pay

New doors all around
And the windows were found
To all need to be replaced
And the hickory plank
On the floor broke the bank
When the bill I finally faced
The cost of each part
Tore at my heart
And I saw large bills with wings
I suffered huge strife
With my generous wife
When she called for extra things

Throughout the ordeal
We were made to feel
That Bennett really cares
About this place
And that he was the ace

When it comes to mountain bears
But 'twas really John
Who worked on and on
Who ran the whole difficult show
And t'is him we must thank
For each board and plank
But I wish the job weren't so slow!

There are strange things done
In the blazing sun
By the men of Arrowhead
And the mansions there
Will make you swear
And sometimes wish you were dead
When the fierce wind screams
And the water seems
To enter every crack
And the ceiling drips
And your footing slips ,
And you fall down on your back.

Jouni's Ladies

Both Susan and I are very busy, so we eat out often. One of the restaurants we loved was Jouni's, in Upland, near our hangars. It's gone now. It offered many options for sides, etc., with each entre. Many of the patrons were old pilots, like me, who had a hard time making up their minds with regards to which side dishes they wanted.

Home fries, hash browns, cottage cheese or fruit...
Doot Doot Doodely Do
White, wheat, sourdought or biscuit....
What may I serve you?

I wish you would make up your mind
I wish you would stop wastin' my time
If you'd just tell me, I'd be fine

Doot Doot Doodely Do

Home fries, hash browns, fruit or cottage cheese....
Doot doot doodely Do
Can you tell me what you'd like please...
What can I get for you?

Will you please just decide
Which one you'd like for a side
Before I quit and walk outside

Doot Doot Doodely Do

Estate Sale Sadness

Lake Arrowhead, May 25, 2022.

Susan is back from an estate sale. My heart is heavy. Not because of the money she spent, but because of what she bought so cheaply. Beautiful handmade quilts—$15 each. Someone's granny spent several days making every one of them. A little carved wooden bear—$2. Somebody, maybe in China, or Vietnam, or maybe Columbia, spend a day, maybe more, carefully shaping his features. A tiny book of prayers presented "To my Dear Mother" and signed and dated in 1906. The sales lady gave it to Susan. A lovely pitcher, and matching relish plate, $7 for both. They were in a display case, so were someone's treasured antiques, once. Maybe that person is gone now. We can't know.

In my hangar bathroom, I have a made-in-China paper towel holder. I think it cost $2.98. Some poor Chinese person spend at least a couple of hours putting it together. He/she probably got 17 cents for it.

We owe a huge debt to the people that give us everything around us. For every spoon, table, writing pen, building, car, safety pin—everything that was produced for our benefit, by another person. A tiny piece of the soul of whoever builds anything is embedded in that item. Some may not care about what they are making, what they do is just a job. Some deeply care about what they make, like Granny knitting a coverlet for grandbaby. But care or not, a tiny bit of the maker's soul is in their handiwork.

I know that this is not a proper thought for a Christian minister, but I believe everything, everything in the universe, has a soul. Humans probably have the largest, most complicated

souls. My doggie certainly has a soul. So do my airplanes. And so does everything. For those things that are produced by humans, their souls are inherited from their makers. Just a tiny piece.

So why does the cheap antique pitcher make me sad? Because it and its soul were once a treasured prize of somebody. This person honored the maker of the pitcher by admiring it enough to show it proudly in a display case in his or her home. And to sell it for next to nothing dishonors the soul of the person who made it.

I have the same feeling when I see beautiful airplanes wasting away from neglect at airports all over the country. That plane is the work of many dedicated, smart, hard-working guys. To allow it to go to waste dishonors those guys.

Of course, we can't keep everything. And there comes a time when the proudest airplane should be recycled into Coors cans. But for the heirs of the folks that lived in the house of the estate sale to discard their parent's treasures so cavalierly shows an ingratitude that is truly sad.

My Ex

Sometimes relationships just don't work out. Sad, but we move on.

It was great fun while it lasted
But I knew it wouldn't last
For there's always some new player
In life's sad and jaded cast
And all that's left when the curtain falls
Are our memories of the past.

Petey the Engineer

Collin Rivera was my secretary for 15 years. She moved to Texas for family obligations; I miss her yet. She wrote these two poems for a book we published, "The Petey Papers".

There once was a man named Robin
An engineer—one of the best
He worked tirelessly seven days a week
And he rarely got adequate rest

He lived on a mountain of grandeur
An adept aeronautical ace
His partner in life was Susan, his wife
Who kept up with his frenetic pace

They were 'kept' by a cat named Petey
The 3rd 'person' in this equation
A master of napping
And also milk-lapping
An archetype of the feline persuasion

PHOTO BY SUSAN NEWMAN-HARRISON

A vigil he keeps by the doorway
To inspect guests as they arrive
He sizes them up
(Make sure the door's shut!)
Cuz he's monarch of the inside

In order to placate his penchant
For stalking the birds perched outside
He's given a bed by the fireplace
A rough life that he takes in stride

The projects, they come in a flurry
Emails bounce to & fro
He tries to assist with the typing
Depositing fur as he goes

The house in the mountains is vital
To get work done with minimal hassle
But make no mistake
As you gaze at the lake
That the cat is the king of the castle

Rob the Bear

I work for an attorney.
His name is Rob the Bear.
He's an engineer
and does calculations
and flies planes up in the air

His wife — her name is Susan
The woman is non-stop
She's an artist and a pilot
and she also likes to shop

The office is unusual
Tasks vary from day to day
All is well for Rob the Bear
As long as clients pay

The paper trails are endless
And some days may seem to lag
But the fun parts include plane rides
And driving the Corvette and the Jag

We keep the business coming in
from Boeing and Mac Dac
To make sure that commercial airlines
are safely flown intact

The moral of this story is
our well-oiled machine
Must have all parts working in harmony
and running at full steam
Communication is vital and
   our mission here is clear
Vehicular offenders must pay the price
And planes stay in the air.

PHOTO BY LEE CALKINS

Animals I Have Known

My earliest memory of a pet is from when my family—then just my mom Jane, my stepdad Chief Warrant Officer Harrison, USN, and me—lived in Rhode Island. He was a handsome German Shepherd named "Gunner"—in honor of a dog from a book about a USN Patrol Bomber "Y" nicknamed Dumbo— "Gunner and the Dumbo". If you look up this title on Google, you will see that it is selling for as much as $405.00! I remember some things about Rhode Island, but not too much. I was in kindergarten through second grade, as I recall. I do remember that the two crabby old women teachers at the Navy-run school didn't like me and didn't like it when I tried to talk about my Gunner. I figured they weren't too bright, either of them. One told the other, in response to one of my classmates stabbing another classmate with a pencil, that she worried that the stabbed kid could get lead poisoning from the lead pencil. Even at age 7, I knew the lead in a pencil was graphite. Gunner and I were inseparable. Rain or shine, nice weather or snow, every morning he would walk me to the school bus stop and meet me there every afternoon when I escaped the clutches of the two mean old women. He was expert at chasing and retrieving a tossed tennis ball, but he quickly caught on if I pretended to throw a ball when there was none. I swore that he knew how to raise an eyebrow to let me know that he didn't think this was humorous.

When Chief Warrant Officer Harrison was transferred to NAS Memphis, we couldn't take Gunner and had to leave him with a neighbor who helped with him anyhow, as I recall. I think that was the first time I had a broken heart.

After the move to Memphis, I wheedled my poor mom in to going to the pound to look for a dog for me. A smallish mixed-breed shaggy individual, black in hue, came galloping to his cage door and enthusiastically licked my fingers when I approached. This was my dog! We named him "Blackie", and I loved him dearly. Blackie had the bad habit of rushing everywhere, and on a tragic occasion, when I opened the front door, he raced out into the street, and got hit by a car. When I tried to bring him off the street, he instinctively bit my hand, and passed away shortly after. I remember being heartbroken, again.

After 4 years in Memphis, Chief Warrant Officer Harrison was assigned to "Kwaj", also known as "The Rock", Kwajalein Island, in the Marshalls. I believe he was XO (Executive Officer) of the Navy unit there. Because of its remoteness and austerity, even though it was not really at sea, it was classified as Sea Duty. So family couldn't accompany. My mother and two sisters, the youngest of whom was a baby, moved to Los Altos Hills, California. From somewhere or someone we acquired a cat, eponymously named "Mincemeat".

My first car, which lived in the garage there, was a 49 Oldsmobile with a flat-head six motor. It gets pretty cool in the winter in Los Altos Hills; Mincemeat was an outside cat, but she had a secret way of getting into the garage. She somehow got up on top of the warm motor of the Olds. I went out one brisk morning to start off to school, and upon first engine crank heard a horrible blood-curdling yowl. Fortunately, the engine did not start. I rushed to open up the hood and saw that Mince had rested her head on the fan pully, and her neck was now compressed between fan belt and said pulley. I grabbed the fan, backed it off, and freed the poor kitty. She took off like a bat out of Hell, and we didn't see her for a week. I thought that I had inadvertently killed her. But, back she came, skinny but pregnant! So we gave her extra rations, welcomed her babies when they arrived, and gave them all to loving homes. Or at least that is how I would like to remember it. She lived a long and happy life, and continued in her profession as an expert mouser for many years. When she finally went to Kitty Heaven, we adopted "Mincemeat Tooth", tooth as in the second. About this time I went off to college, so of her I haven't much recollection.

My mother Jane had Pomeranians. My memory is hazy, but I think the first one was named Fiddlesticks; a pretty black, as I recall. Legend has it that she (or he?) got eaten by Mr. Coyote on a vacation trip to Yosemite. I was away at school, but it was clear from her phone call that my mom was terribly bereaved by this awful event. Much later, she got another another Pom: I can't remember much about this one. I think this little dog stayed until Jane passed away. Probably the older of my sisters took her.

About the time of the ill-fated Yosemite trip, my stepdad Harry, now no longer CWO Harrison, retired from the Navy, had purchased a Weimaraner puppy. This dog was a purebred and very expensive. Harry was an avid upland bird hunter. This kind of hunting requires a well-trained dog to flush the birds out of hiding, and to retrieve the birds from where they fall. Weimaraners are supposed to be very good at this sort of thing. Harry's dog had along Prussian string of names but he was colloquially known as "Tannenbaum", or "Tannen" for short, because he came into our lives on Christmas day.

Tannen was well trained for a young dog; he won the "puppy class" Weimaraner field trials. Harry was very proud of his dog, even though Tannen performed much better as a cute puppy than as a working hunter's helper. But he was a wonderful companion for Harry, and went with him almost everywhere. And though he lived in a snug kennel behind the house, he was often found snoozing in front of the fire.

Harry was tragically killed in an auto accident in about 1973. Of course the dog was disconsolate. I was away working for the Forest Service, so I couldn't take him. Jane had her Pomeranian, and just couldn't manage a big hunting dog. So Tannen went to a long-time hunting buddy who had been on hunts with Harry and the dog.

I like to say that I have always had at least one pet. That may be true, but I think there were gaps. At least there are gaps in my memory. There was a cat that joined us when my first wife Christine and baby Janie moved from Corvallis, where I had just graduated from Oregon State College, to Los Angeles. I went to work at what was then called the Motor Vehicle Pollution Control Board, now the Air Resources Board. I can't remember how we got her, I think maybe she just walked in off the street. My daughter Janie named her "Sweety", maybe, but I'm not sure that is accurate. In any event, she stayed with us when we moved through a couple of rentals, and on to Pomona. We rented a house on Dudley Street, which at the time so many years ago was in a very nice neighborhood. The neighborhood isn't so nice anymore.

Two or three years later, shortly after I went to work at the Forest Service, we somehow ended up with a Samoyed named Cobber. This dog was impossible! He humped EVERY leg he could ever find. We had a lovely fenced yard, which he managed to dig his way out of dozens and dozens of times. He howled like the huskies in Robert Service's "The Cremation of Sam Magee".

I honestly don't know what became of him, I suspect we may have foisted him off on some other unsuspecting family. We had Sweety the cat, there too, as I recall. I know she presented us with at least one litter of kittens, and I suspect we found homes for at least most of them. Not much memory of Sweety—but I think Christine took her after our divorce.

I had no pets for a while, after the divorce. There was a mutt dog, "Mercator" who owned Ed, the best man at my wedding to Deborah I. He lived at the airplane shop Ed and I shared; the dog and I were friends but not close.

And then there were Doxie, Honeybun, and Rugby Rabbit. My girlfriend at the time had a Jack Russel Terrier, named Doxie. She was a great little dog, full of mischief and enthusiasm. One morning I was assigned to take Doxie out for her A M walk. We had a nice stroll in the park across the street, where there were some lovely mud puddles. Of course, the Dox absolutely had to splash and shake, and managed to adhere several ounces of clay mud to her paws. Needless to say, I took some abuse after she dirtied all the rugs in the apartment.

But Doxie passed away, and was replaced by a bunny named Honeybun. Girlfriend had honeybun for couple years, but rabbits don't live too long, and she left us. Having had a good relationship with the bunny, we decided to get another rabbit. Honeybun succumbed to female difficulties, or so the vet said. So we decided that we needed a boy rabbit. The pet store dude said—yes—this is a boy rabbit. So Rugby came home with us. He was a really tough customer—he roamed all around the fenced back yard, defying any other animal to trespass on his yard. The only thing that scared him was when a bird's shadow crossed the yard, he was absolutely terrified of hawks, it seems.

I was negotiating a construction defect settlement in Century City, perhaps 60 miles from home. Girlfriend called in a panic— "Rugby is sick!" Me-"So, take him to the vet!" Well, turns out that Rug was having the monthly in-heat episode. He, though identifying as a male, was really a girl rabbit. After girlfriend left in a huff one late night, and I sold the Claremont house where Rugby and I lived, Rugby went to live with one of my employee's grandmother, who had always wanted a rabbit.

He/she was a good little friend, and I hated to give him/her up, but I had too much on my plate to give the attention he/she deserved.

Another dog came into my life briefly, "Buster". My wife Susan and I were driving along Cajon Blvd, and we spotted Buster, obviously very thirsty, trotting along the road. I said "that dog is in trouble—we gotta go back" "OK", said Susan. We pulled up next to him and I said "Get in the car." He got right in. I cut the bottom off of a plastic water bottle to make a little bowl and gave him a drink. He drank about a quart, poor puppy.

I struggled with what to do with him, as I certainly didn't want him going back to guarding the marijuana plantation he escaped from. (I speculate). So, I took him to the Pomona Shelter, which advertises they are "no-kill", and tearfully dropped him off. Two weeks later I called to see if I could adopt him, he was already adopted, or so the kid on the phone said. I flagellate myself to this day for turning him over to the government, I should have taken him home.

Susan had Powder the cockatoo, a white, very affectionate bird. We both loved Powder. But she didn't take to the move to the mountains well at all, shrieked constantly, and so we decided that she should go to the Magnolia Bird Farm, where she could be properly cared for. Maybe that wasn't the right thing to do, but at the time it felt like it was.

And then there was Wally. He was and is a huge galumphing slobbering bulldog puppy, whose mom is Susan's glamorous girlfriend Jill. We babysat him for a whole week, during which time he became very attached to me, and I to him. When Jill and husband Craig came to reclaim him, he didn't want to go! I cried a little when he left.

There are a couple other dogs I should have done more to help, but time and circumstance prevented. One was a small fluffy white guy, maybe a Maltese. He was obviously hurt, and begging for someone to take him to the vet. I was late to a medical appointment, and when I went back he was gone. I pray that some person was a better Samaritan than I was.

The second was a poor old dog with a terrible cancer on his neck. He was in the yard at the store where I get welding supplies. A stray, not attached to the store. I was reluctant to approach him too closely, he was very shy and skittish. Maybe if I had been more patient, I might have coaxed him to come, and gotten him to the vet, so he could have had at least a painless exit.

And Diego, a boxer mix, who lived in a fenced yard at the "bottom of the hill" (Lake Arrowhead jargon for anyplace except Lake Arrowhead.) I stopped to give him treats whenever I drove by. He was very grateful. There were later two little white woofers in the yard with him, one escaped, and I put him back in. And the feral cats—who lived at the fire station next to Diego's house. I gave them cat food every day. Sadly enough, Diego and friends aren't there anymore, and some bureaucrat, I suspect, rounded up all my cats. I miss them.

Then, we got Petey. Or, Petey got us. Petey legally belonged to Tim, a dear airport friend and an all-around animal lover. Tim was a house painter, and always had a large pile of tarps in the back of his truck. He was surprised to uncover Petey, then just a baby kitten, hidden in his tarps. Mrs. Tim being violently allergic to cats, Petey was established

as an airport resident. One cold evening, he wandered into my hangar, and lay down in front of the heater I had going. I took him home, for just that one night, or at least that is what I planned. But he ended up with Susan and me. I refer you, Gentle Reader, to "The Petey Papers", Petey's autobiographic novel. His full story is much too long to relate here.

Couple stories of non-pet animals. One was a very brave gopher who attacked me at the Dudley house. Our landlady had caught him in a trap, and pulled the trap up, and shrieked that Ms. Gopher was getting away, I had to kill her. Which I regretfully did. I feel guilty even yet. I had never killed an animal, even a mouse or a rat.

There was an assortment of lizards, birds, snakes, and so forth that I dispatched unknowingly. One little lizard got caught up in the hangar door, I amputated his tail and one foot. He soldiered on, I saw him some time later, he looked pretty fat for a disabled veteran.

One bird who flew into my 1955 Plymouth Fury maybe 60 years ago. I remember her/him because my girlfriend at the time remonstrated with me for displaying tears over killing a bird—"It's just a bird." Broke up with her shortly after that.

Another one was a raven. He was a youngster, just about to fly. He was kicked out of his nest, by either a sibling or a parent, and he landed on my hangar floor. I should have captured him, taken him up to Arrowhead, given him something to eat, and he would have been my buddy forever. But I didn't try hard enough to get him, he hopped away, and the other ravens killed him. My friend Tim, from whom we stole Petey, tried to save him, but to no avail. In my memory, he is on my deck rail, and answers to the name of "Nevermore."

And now there is Little Bear. For years, in quiet moments, I would mumble "I want a dog". Susan was doing business with a city person in Apple Valley one afternoon, and the lady she was seeing had her dog with her in the office. Susie: "Oh what a beautiful dog! My husband wants a dog." "Well," said the lady, "she came from the shelter just down the street. Why don't you go there?" Susan had been looking in the various shelters around, but hadn't clicked with any dogs. This dog at the shelter looked just right to her. There was a problem, the dog was chipped, and the two-week waiting period had not quite run. Plus, there was a couple, the wife was blind, who also wanted this particular dog.

On adoption day, lots were drawn, and Susan got the high number. The husband was quite annoyed, but the wife told Susan "God wanted you to have this dog!" So, the dog was on her way to her forever home. The poor pup's fur was so matted up and stuck with cockleburs that whenever she sat down, she cried. Susan took her to the groomer, and she got a U S Marine Corps baldy shave. She was pretty skinny, and pretty shy.

Susan brought her in in her crate, and set the crate on the couch, and opened the door. Then she called me up from my office downstairs, I was working. It was love at first sight. Little Bear came right over to me, and I picked her up, and it was crystal clear that she was gonna be my doggie.

She is anything but a perfect pet—very demanding, barks loudly whenever she wants anything, inserts herself between Susan and me whenever we try to hug, and turns her nose up at anything but the most expensive dog food.

Because she had a big German Shepherd named Greta for a roommate at the shelter, she thinks she is a big dog. She snarks and barks at other dogs and chases off dogs that are five times her size. She growls and nips at little kids who try to pet her. I'm working

PHOTO BY PETER MURRAY

Little Bear on the flightline, Planes of Fame Air Show, Chino, CA.

on this behavior, but maybe not making much progress.

But on the positive side, she is an extremely alert intruder alarm. She lets us know if anybody, even a squirrel, shows up at any of our doors. She patrols the yard where she exercises and lets us know if Mr. Bear or Ms. Racoon and family have been by for a visit. She is very smart.

One evening we were taking a little walk, and Mr. and Mrs. Bear and their two teenagers came sauntering up the driveway. This is not unusual in Arrowhead– we have bobcats, deer, mountain lions, eagles, after all, it is their forest. She let out a mighty bark, and headed for the door full throttle, urging me to get inside. She is very protective of me and Susan, and won't let any other dog get close without challenging him/her. She throws an absolute tantrum if either Susan or I try to leave in a car without her. When we take her, she rides in the back seat, quiet like a little mousie. And when only one of us has to leave, she waits at the front door for hours until that person gets home.

Whenever she is bad, which is often, Susan says to me "You wanted a dog!" Yes, I did. But I couldn't imagine my life without her now.

You can read about Little Bear and her boyfriend in her story book "Little Bear and Brutus".

Apologies to the Blacksmith

One of the best-known poems in the English language is Longfellow's "The Village Blacksmith". Here is a parody on that famous poem, substituting a fat, lazy kitty for the brawny blacksmith.

Under a pretty rose-bush tree
My old cat does rest
A fat and lazy dude is he
Sleep's what he does best
Unless he wants a snack for free
And then he doth protest.

The cat is very handsome,
But he's not the perfect pet
He demands food for ransom
For the snuggles you might get
And then he'll purr and carry on
In ways you can't forget.

His fur is soft, his tail is long
Has lovely amber eyes
But when he's asked to come along
You're in for a surprise
For then he yowls loud and strong
And pitifully he cries.

Thanks, thanks to thee, my chubby cat
For the lessons thou have taught
Like when I try to trim your nails
My efforts come to naught
And trying to give you medicine
With difficulty's fraught.

The Real Petey

If you have read "The Petey Papers", you would know Petey is a famous brave but kind and considerate nobleman. However, sometimes one's public image is not entirely accurate.

Having been owned by Petey for several years now, and especially since the below mentioned Battle of Arrowhead won all Arrowhead Cats nearly unlimited food as an entitlement, we have developed a more realistic view of "our" cat. This poem illustrates a more mature attitude toward Petey.

If you can make a yeowl when all
  are shushing you
And stalk away while never looking back
If you can terrify the dog that's crushing you
Or cough a hairball up while going "gack"
If you can scorn the folks that most adore you
And pee where it can never be cleaned up
If you can rip the ones who just abhor you
Be they human, kitty cat, or pup.

If you can catch a rat, chipmunk, or mouse
And torture it nearly to its end
Then present it to the lady of the house
As a present that you are proud to send
If you can sit up on your mistress' desk top
And always get directly in her way

PHOTO BY SUSAN NEWMAN-HARRISON

And jump and roll and prance and
  only flip flop
When you, and not your humans,
  want to play.

If you will eat only the rarest cat food
Regardless of the price the humans pay
For treats and snacks and stuff to make
  you fat food
And hiss at them when they need to go away
If you refuse to poop where you are
  supposed to
And think that it's all right that you do that
And refuse to let them get too close to
You, then you must be my Petey cat!

ILLUSTRATION BY ALEXUS ELAINE RAISTY

Bear Meals

Shifting our focus to a different animal: Nephew Brennan was assigned to write a poem about a bear using some poetic devices—repetition, allusion, rhyming, and some more as I remember. To encourage him, I wrote this.

I love a black, black bear
You see him every where
He eats what you don't care
About

He scans the garbage cans
His paws look just like hands
Each night the black bear plans
To go out

Routinely eats his find
Nothing specific in mind
He'll survive on any kind
He loves trout

I really like Mr. Bear
I wish that I could wear
A coat like his woolly hair
No doubt

Little Bear's Complaint

The two animals that live here in Summerhill are Petey and Little Bear. They don't get along to well together. See "Abdulla Bulbul Ameer", by William Percy French.

PHOTO BY SUSAN NEWMAN-HARRISON

She lived in a big house with Petey the Cat
She didn't like him all that much
Cause the cat would climb up,
and push out the pup
From the mom that she most liked to touch.

This cat, it would seem,
was always quite mean
And wanted never to share
The spot on the floor,
by the living room door
Where the sun would radiate there.

So she barked, and she snarked,
and she growled and she whined
And she howled like a great outdoor wolf
But the cat didn't care,
he continued right there,
Remaining completely aloof.

She went on eBay, and tried right away
To place in an ad for the cat
But her parents found out,
and they both did shout
"You just can't do that, you brat."

The daughters of Bichon were pretty and lean
And most were exceedingly fair
But the fanciest pup of the lot it would seem
Was a dog who was named Little Bear.

She was playful and loving as all Bichons are
And loyal to her dad to the end
She best liked a ride in the new Bentley car
And she had Brutus Dog as a friend.

L. Bear, to this day, has not got her way
To exclusively lie in that spot
Petey prevails, and Doggie still rails,
And complains about it a lot.

There is plenty of sun, and really no one
Can claim to own it at all
But the puppy is mad, and seems very sad
And just turns her face to the wall.

Not a Lone Dog

"Lone Dog" by Irene McLeod is about a rough, tough, independent dog. Little Bear is not a Lone Dog.

PHOTO BY DEE HUNTER

ILLUSTRATION BY GARY RAINSBARGER

I'm a small dog, not a tall dog, a fluffy dog, and white
I like to think I'm very fierce, but never ever bite
I'm a waggy dog, a braggy dog, I love to snuggle up
And hear you tell me that you think that I'm the perfect pup.

I'll never be an outdoor dog, eating mice and rats
I love to run around the house, and tease the silly cats
I love the toasty fireside—The dogfood that I eat
I love to lie beside my dad, and cuddle at his feet.

I don't mind the other dogs, visiting a while
I love the groomer lady, who makes me up in style
Not for me the lone, hard trail—that's a bunch of bull
But fancy clothes, and special treats, and food bowl always full.

40

Sandburg Cat

I don't think too highly of Carl Sandburg, but as a poet it is clear he enjoys more fame than I ever will. So here is a parody on his famous "Fog".

PHOTO BY SUSAN NEWMAN-HARRISON

The cat comes on little cat feet
It sits looking over the feeding bowl
on silent haunches
And then moves on

Vampire Cat

A poet I do think very highly of is Rudyard Kipling. So, this parody on his "The Vampire".

A cat there was and his name was Pete
Oh what a terrible cat
He had a long tail and great big feet
Everyone thought he was really neat
But all he ever did was eat
Oh what a terrible cat!

The vet had said that diet he must
Oh what a terrible cat
But all the vet got was a look of disgust
Vets are people you just can't trust
I'll just eat until I bust,
Oh what a terrible cat.

Oh the crackers we waste
And the snackers we waste
And the food we try to withhold
Belong to the cat that does nothing but eat
Who will whine for hours for a treat
Until we just have to fold.

The cat ate until he became very fat
Oh what a terrible cat
He looked more like a large furry hat
Than a sleek feline who chases the rat
And terrifies poor mousie at that
Oh what a terrible cat.

Oh lord how I've tried and tried and tried
Oh what a terrible cat
To cut down his food so he won't be so wide
I've pleaded and begged and even cried
But the cat simply howls
  with his mouth open wide
Oh what a terrible cat.

ILLUSTRATION BY ALEXUS ELAINE RAISTY

Autumn Leaves

Here is a short poem about the fat kitty. Sung to the tune "Autumn Leaves"

The chubby cat
Sits on my desk top
The chubby cat
Of black and brown

He licks his paws
And taps his tail
And prances 'round
like he's a clown

But what he really wants
Is just a yummy
Treat, of catnip leaf
To fill his tummy

And though I feed you every day, my kitty
You eat the most of all
When I let yummy treats fall.

A Fat Cat's Lament

Even Petey himself realizes he needs to lose a little weight. Sung to the tune of "Oh, I don't look good naked any more"

Oh I'm not a skinny kitty any more
All I do is lie around and snore
If I keep on like this,
I won't get through my pet door
Oh I'm not a handsome kitty any more.

I used to be a hell of a cat
I could catch every squirrel, mouse and rat
And rip their guts out in 2 seconds flat
And never eat enough to make me fat.

I know they want to put me on a diet
I just dare them to go ahead and try it
I will raise all hell and cause a riot
Cause I like being sleepy nice and quiet.

PHOTO BY SUSAN NEWMAN-HARRISON

Col. Petey

Petey's address to his troops before the battle of Lake Arroehead—If you have read "The Petey Papers", you will know that Petey has had a distinguished military career—rising to the rank of Colonel. He commanded the Cat Force in their triumphant defeat of the humans of Lake Arrowhead. Robert Burns "Scots Wha Hae".

ILLUSTRATION BY ALEXUS ELAINE RAISTY

Cats wha wish to stay in bed
Cats wham no one ever lead
Cats wha demand to be fed
Sleep for half the day!

Now's the day and now's the time
Cats whose meow shall loudly chime
Cats wha's treatment is a crime
Rise, and go and play!

Wha would tolerate a dog
Wha would hide behind a log
Wha would shy from cow or hog
Let him be away!

Wha for kittie's life and law
Wha shall bare his fiercest paw
Wha shall sharpen every claw
We shall win the fray!

By the humans wha oppress
By the brats that make us dress
We shall end this sorry mess
Before we go astray.

Scratch their eyes out, one by one!
Puke on their rugs, just for fun!
When they come, get up and run!
Cats rule, and this shall be!

(Be is pronounced "bay" in the Scots dialect)

The Recycling Lizard

My wife is a marketing specialist, and one of her clients was the county Recycling Department. Here is a short poem I wrote, but the bureaucrats didn't like it, and it was never used. My sister is named Lizzy, and she loved it.

Oh I am the recycling lizard
My friends they all call me Lizzy
I recycle everything, you may have heard,
That 's why I am always so busy.

You can help us save the earth
You can make a difference
You can give it all you're worth
Don' t sit on the recycling fence.

Put your bottles and paper and cans
In the proper blue recycling box
Tell this to your all friends and fans
Tell it to the desert rats and the fox.

Tell it to the birds and to the bugs
Tell it to the desert folks near and far
Then John will give you great big hugs
And you will be a recycling star!

Poem for Brennan

Brennan is my best and favorite nephew. The quotes are sentences he was assigned (3rd grade maybe?) to punctuate and correct spelling. He completed the assignment with a grade of 100%. I am very proud of him. At eight years old, Brennan was already driving the motorized lawn mower. His Dad is a US Marine. Here's a poem for Brennan, my bud...

I have a friend named Brennan
He's really quite a scholar!
10 out of 10 on his last test
Made his mother holler.

"I have nine dimes"
Well writ said the prof!
But I say only nine?
Times must be pretty tough!

"Put the fish in the bath"
Poor fish-he hates the bubbles
He'd rather go in the ocean
That would end all his troubles.

"Jake will make a cake"
That's a great break for Jake
I hope it's made with chocolate!
And Jake's mom helps him bake.

"The snapping turtle bit my friend"
"I live in the jungle" too
"I can sing a song" as well
I would love to sing with you!

"I ate the big pickle"
Sounds like Hemingway
"My cousin giggles at my jokes"
She's kind of strange that way.

So, Brennan, you Irish Marine
You skier, driver, and bard
I say to you "Semper Fi"
And keep on pushing hard.

Ivan Skavinsky Skivar

*And a little clip, in the style of French,
Brennan reminds us of Ivan Skavinsky Skivar!*

There was talent aplenty in the Flannagan clan
And Brennan was one of the best.
He made the dean's list
While his buddies all pissed,
and he could even play chess!

PHOTOS BY SUSAN NEWMAN-HARRISON

Pretty Girl

Helen is a producer/proofreader/publisher. We met her and showed her a couple of my poems which she claimed to like. We have lost track of her—sad.

We met a pretty girl last week
One we would like to know.
She claims to be a Senior
But I doubt that it is so.

Tall, lithe, and full of fun,
A skilled conversationalist,
A wonderful sense of the appropriate,
But no single detail missed.

For all her outward pulchritude
And all her writing skill
Its what's inside, Suz agrees,
That makes her lovelier still.

She liked my poems!

I'm glad to hear
that you were smitten
by the poem
that I have written.

When my Dad
was here on Earth
we'd correspond
for what it's worth,

In rhyme alone
and limerick
But all HIS rhymes
Would make you sick!

The UPS Man

My son, knowing I have pretensions of being a poet, sent me a T-shirt with Poe's "The Raven" on it.

Once upon a morning weary
While I struggled, weak and weary
over many an arcane and obscure legal brief.

Suddenly then was I suprised
By UPS man, I surmised
So went I doorwise, with relief.

For so bored I was that I
Was very happy to comply
With his banging on the door.

And what he had yes, was a shirt
the color of mountain dirt
And with my fav'rite, Nevermore!

Dogwood

There are many wonderful things about living in Lake Arrowhead: It is cool in the summer, we have snowy winters, the people who live here are always friendly and cordial, there are many fine dogs and cats who live here. The forest and lake are beautiful and inspiring. One of the best things is the profusion of lovely dogwood trees. Here is a little story about them.

Pine and Dogwood lived in a beautiful forest, overlooking a lovely lake. Oak lived there, too. Oak was very, very old. And Fir, Big Cone, and Manzanita also lived there. The big trees didn't think too much of Manzanita, but that is a story for another time.

One day Pine said to Dogwood "Dogwood, Oak told me that when he was just an acorn, his great great grandpa told him that Dogwood was once the straightest, strongest tree in the forest. Your trunk and branches are crooked and weak. What happened?"

Dogwood replied "Oh, Pine, I am so ashamed. Many, many years ago, when the Romans decided to crucify Christ, they knew He was the king of the Jews, and so out of respect they sought the straightest, strongest tree they could find. It was Dogwood. When Dogwood learned this, he was so ashamed. He prayed to God to make his trunk and branches weak and crooked, so he could never, never again be used for such a terrible thing. He prayed and prayed, and God answered him. God said "Dogwood, do not be ashamed. You have done nothing wrong. But I will grant your prayer, your trunk and branches shall forevermore be weak and crooked.

"But Dogwood," God said, "do not grieve. My son Jesus shall rise again, from the dead, to save the souls of everyone who believes in me. And to help you remind all the people of my promise, I will make you have the most beautiful flowers in the forest. Some shall be red, to remind of the blood Christ shed.

PHOTO BY SUSAN NEWMAN-HARRISON

Some shall be yellow, to remind of the tears of Mary. Some shall be pure white, to remind of the purity of my love for you. And the most beautiful shall be white, with rust colored spots on the edge of each petal, to remind of the nails used to crucify my son, and the suffering he endured, to assure all who believe a place with Him."

Pine answered "Dogwood, thank you for that story. You need not be ashamed, but be joyful. You do indeed have the most beautiful flowers in the forest, and now I see what important work you are doing. May God bless you, and bless us all."

Mamas Don't Let Your Babies Be Pilots

With abject apologies to Waylon Jennings, modified to the present situation. "Zulu" is pilot talk for coordinated universal time, formerly Greenwhich Mean Time. Since pilots find themselves in several time zones every day, this avoids confusion. "Bag" is pilot talk for Nomex flight suit.

Pilots ain't easy to love and they're harder to hold.
They'd rather talk about flying than give diamonds and gold.
Lycoming belt buckles and olive drab flight suits
And every morning he looks at the sky
And thinks only 'bout the plane he will fly
an' if he's a test pilot, and he don't die young,
He'll prob'ly just fly away.

Mamas, don't let your babies grow up to be pilots
Don't let 'em hang out at the airport an' sweep hangers for time
Let 'em be mechanics and dispatchers and such.
Mamas don't let your babies grow up to be pilots
'Cos they'll never stay home and they'll always be flying
An' love their airplane more than anyone else.

Pilots like airport cafes, where old pilots go
And to talk about engines, and spinning, and yesterday's crash
Them that don't fly won't like him and them that do,
Sometimes wish he'd shut up about airplanes
He ain't wrong, he's just different but his pride won't let him,
Abandon his flying, even when he should.

Mamas, don't let your babies grow up to be pilots.
Don't let 'em wear that olive drab bag, with patches from his squadron
And a great big wristwatch that has Zulu and Standard,
Mamas don't let your babies grow up to be pilots.
'Cos they'll never stay home and they're always alone.
Even in an airplane with someone they love.

Oh Bear Oh Bear Oh Bear

Finally, here is an apology to my poor wife. She puts up with, and even encourages, my foolish behavior. An 81 year old has no business flying airshows, racing a Corvette, working full time, but because of Susan's help and support, I can still do these things. Thank you beautiful Susan!

Oh bear oh bear oh bear oh bear
What are you doing Bear?
You're an old and feeble bear
You should be sitting in your chair
Watching Oprah (that's not fair)
Oh bear oh bear oh bear.

Oh bear oh bear oh bear oh bear
Why are you doing this?
Why are you driving thru the mist?
It only makes your poor wife pissed!
It only puts you on her list
Oh bear oh bear oh bear.

Oh bear oh bear oh bear oh bear
Why did you buy another plane?
Why do you fly it in the rain?
Why do you cause your poor wife pain?
You are way too old, it is plain
Oh bear oh bear oh bear.

Oh bear oh bear oh bear oh bear
Why are you going down the hill
When you know that you are ill
When you know you need to take a pill
When you know your coffee you will spill
Oh bear oh bear oh bear.

Oh bear oh bear oh bear oh bear
I guess that is just the way
That a bear gonna spend his day, his day
Always at work, and never at play
Don't matter what his poor wife say
Oh bear oh bear oh bear.

PHOTO BY SUSAN NEWMAN-HARRISON

PHOTO BY ERIC VAN GILDER

PHOTO BY ROBERT SPELLMAN

Rob Harrison, ZLIN 50LS.

About The Author

Robin T. Harrison, P.E.

Rob and his wife Susan live in a house with a three hundred sixty degree view on top of a mountain in the resort community of Lake Arrowhead, fifty miles east of Los Angeles, California. Here they share space with Little Bear and Petey the cat.

Rob is an aeronautical engineer, a registered safety engineer, a retired lawyer, and a professional airshow stunt pilot. He enjoys maintaining and modifying his own aircraft. He spent thirty years with the U S Forest Service, starting as a fire fighter in Oregon and retiring as Program Leader for Aviation at the San Dimas Technology and Development Center in Southern California.